W9-AUU-869

Pebble® Plus

LET'S LOOK AT COUNTRIES

LET'S LOOK AT THE

UNITED STATES OF AMERICA

BY JOY FRISCH-SCHMOLL

CAPSTONE PRESS
a capstone imprint

Pebble Plus is published by Capstone Press,
1710 Roe Crest Drive, North Mankato, Minnesota 56003
www.mycapstone.com

Library of Congress Cataloging-in-Publication Data
Names: Reynolds, A. M., 1958– author.
Title: Let's look at the United States of America / by A.M. Reynolds.
Description: North Mankato, Minnesota : Pebble Plus, an imprint of Capstone Press, 2019. | Series: Pebble plus. Let's look at countries
Identifiers: LCCN 2018029933 (print) | LCCN 2018032738 (ebook) | ISBN 9781977103918 (eBook PDF) | ISBN 9781977103826 (hardcover) | ISBN 9781977105615 (pbk.)
Subjects: LCSH: United States--Juvenile literature.
Classification: LCC E156 (ebook) | LCC E156 .R48 2019 (print) | DDC 973—dc23
LC record available at https://lccn.loc.gov/2018029933

Editorial Credits
Erika L. Shores, editor; Juliette Peters, designer;
Jo Miller, media researcher; Laura Manthe, production specialist

Photo Credits
Getty Images: Hisham Ibrahim, 17, John Fedele, 13; Newscom: Blend Images/Deborah Kolb, 11; Shutterstock: Allen.G, 8, Andreas C. Fischer, Cover Bottom, Cover Back, Artush, 9, Globe Turner, 22 (Inset), kojihirano, 21, mandritoiu, Cover Top, Mariusz S. Jurgielewicz, 6, nate, 4, Nitr, 19, Orhan Cam, 5, Patrick Tr, 7, Peter Kunasz, 22-23, 24, Songquan Deng, 1, 15, Steve Collender, Cover Middle, Stuart Monk, 3

Note to Parents and Teachers

The Let's Look at Countries set supports national curriculum standards for social studies related to people, places, and culture. This book describes and illustrates the United States of America. The images support early readers in understanding the text. The repetition of words and phrases helps early readers learn new words. This book also introduces early readers to subject-specific vocabulary words, which are defined in the Glossary section. Early readers may need assistance to read some words and to use the Table of Contents, Glossary, Read More, Internet Sites, Critical Thinking Questions, and Index sections of the book.

Printed and bound in China.
970

TABLE OF CONTENTS

Where Is the United States of America?

The United States is a country in North America. It is between Canada and Mexico. The capital city is Washington, D.C.

United States of America

Washington, D.C.

From Mountains to Deserts

The country has mountains

in the West and East.

Prairies and hills lie in between.

The Southwest has deserts.

The North is colder than the South.

In the Wild

America has all kinds of wildlife.

U.S. forests are home to deer,

wolves, and bears. Prairie dogs

and bison live on the plains.

Bald eagles are the national bird.

bald eagle

bison

People

The first Americans were Native Americans.

Over time people from other countries

came to the United States.

They brought different languages

and ways of life.

On the Job

Most Americans work in banks, hospitals, and other service jobs. Some work in government. Some workers build airplanes, cars, computers, or houses.

Summer Celebration

The 4th of July is the country's birthday.

People grill food and have picnics.

Marching bands play in parades.

Colorful fireworks fill the night sky.

On the Field

Football is the most watched sport in the United States. People also watch basketball and baseball. Soccer is also popular. Many children play on teams.

Time to Eat

Half of Americans eat burgers,

pizza, or other fast food once a week.

Fries and other potatoes are

the most popular vegetable.

Chicken is the most popular meat.

Famous Site

The Grand Canyon is in the Southwest. It has layers of different colored rocks. Visitors can hike to the bottom.

QUICK UNITED STATES OF AMERICA FACTS

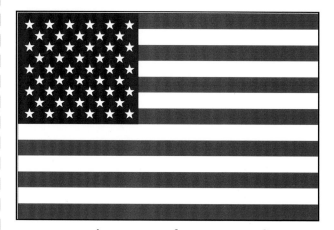

United States of America flag

Name: United States of America

Capital: Washington, D.C.

Other major cities: New York City, Los Angeles, Chicago

Population: 326,625,791 (2017 estimate)

Size: 3,796,742 square miles (9,833,517 sq km)

Language: English, Spanish

Money: U.S. dollar

GLOSSARY

fast food—food from a restaurant that is made and served very quickly

government—the group of people who make laws, rules, and decisions for a country or state

plain—a large, flat area of land with few trees

popular—liked or enjoyed by many people

prairie—a large area of flat or rolling grassland with few or no trees

READ MORE

Gilbert, Sara. *American Food.* Cooking School. Mankato, Minn.: Creative Education, 2015.

Kopp, Megan. *United States.* Countries. New York: Smartbook Media Inc., 2018.

Waters, Kate. *Where the Buffalo Roam: Bison in America.* New York: Penguin Young Readers, 2017.

INTERNET SITES

Use FactHound to find Internet sites related to this book.

Visit *www.facthound.com*

Just type 9781977103826 and go.

 Check out projects, games and lots more at
www.capstonekids.com

CRITICAL THINKING QUESTIONS

1. Describe the different types of landforms in the United States.

2. What are some wild animals that live in the area where you live?

3. Which sport or game is your favorite?

INDEX